Contemporary African Americans

COLIN POWELL

BY
DIANE PATRICK-WEXLER

RSVP
**RAINTREE
STECK-VAUGHN**
P U B L I S H E R S
The Steck-Vaughn Company

Austin, Texas

Published by Raintree Steck-Vaughn, an imprint of Steck-Vaughn Company.
Produced by Mega-Books, Inc.
Design and Art Direction by Michaelis/Carpelis Design Associates.
Cover photo: ©E. Adams/Sygma.

Library of Congress Cataloging-in-Publication Data
Patrick-Wexler, Diana.
    Colin Powell/by Diane Patrick-Wexler.
        p.   cm.—(Contemporary African Americans)
    Includes bibliographical references and index.
    Summary: Traces the life of Colin Powell, from his childhood to his success as the first black chairman of the Joint Chiefs of Staff.
    ISBN 0-8172-3977-4 (Hardcover)
    ISBN 0-8114-9797-6 (Softcover)
    1. Powell, Colin L.—Juvenile literature. 2. Generals—United States—Biography—Juvenile literature. 3. Afro-American generals—Biography—Juvenile literature. 4. United States. Army—Biography—Juvenile literature. [1. Powell, Colin L. 2. Generals. 3. Afro-Americans—Biography.]
I. Title. II. Series.
E840.5.P68P38 1996
355'.0092—dc20   95-11153
[B]   CIP
                                                                        AC
Printed and bound in the United States.

    2 3 4 5 6 7 8 9 LB 99 98 97 96

Photo Credits: Woodfin Camp & Associates, Inc.: pp. 4, 11, 15, 16, 27, 29; UPI/Bettmann: pp. 7, 9, 12, 22, 25, 33, 34, 37, 41, 42, 44; Courtesy of The City College of New York/CUNY: p.18; Johnson/Gamma Liaison: p.21; Reuters/Bettmann: p. 31; Jeffrey Markowitz/Sygma: p. 38.

Contents

1 Shooting for the Stars 5

2 Growing Up in the Bronx 8

3 Maturing in the Army 14

4 Winning Respect 19

5 Helping Presidents 28

6 A National Hero 36

Important Dates 46

Glossary 47

Bibliography 47

Index 48

Chapter One

SHOOTING FOR THE STARS

September 1994—U.S. Navy ships and Air Force planes fill the sea and sky. U.S. troops are on their way to invade the island country of Haiti. Their orders are to force Haiti's illegal military government out of power. The violent Haitian military had overthrown the government of the country's elected president, Jean-Bertrand Aristide. Aristide waits in exile in the United States. Haitian soldiers have promised to fight the U.S. **invasion** to the death.

At the last minute, former U.S. President Jimmy Carter tries to negotiate with the Haitian military leaders. It is a dangerous, risky mission. Jimmy Carter knows that General Colin Powell will be of great help. In his thirty years in the military, he has been an excellent problem solver. Jimmy Carter asks General

General Colin L. Powell has served his country in both war and peace.

Powell to join the **negotiating** team on its way to Haiti.

When Powell meets with the Haitian general, Raoul Cedras, he convinces him not to resist when the U.S. troops arrive. President Aristide is restored to power peacefully. Thanks, in part, to Colin Powell, many lives have been saved.

Colin Powell's adult life has been filled with the keeping of peace and the horror of war. But when he was a boy growing up in the South Bronx, Colin did not even know what war was. That soon changed. In college, Powell joined the military and became a soldier. He would see war many times.

Colin Powell was not in the military just to fight. He was curious about history, government, and the ways countries settle their differences. He studied these topics and even went back to school later in life to learn more.

During his military career, Colin's knowledge about history and government earned him many challenging jobs. Several presidents depended on him for military advice. He made history by becoming the first African-American Chairman of the Joint Chiefs of Staff. As the nation's top soldier, he was in charge of all the leaders of the armed forces. Powell helped plan military operations, such as Operation Desert Storm in the Persian Gulf in 1991. Even after he retired in 1993, his skills helped solve the 1994 crisis in Haiti.

Today, General Powell has not forgotten his roots. His hardworking parents had left the island of Jamaica

In 1991, Colin Powell, the nation's top soldier, was honored by the Horatio Alger Association. This group gives awards to people who have started small and gone on to achieve great things.

to build a better life in the United States. "Strive for a good education," was their message to their son. "Make something of your life." At first, Colin was not very interested in school. Even in college he did not know what he wanted to be—until he saw the uniformed **cadets** in the Reserve Officers' Training Corps, or ROTC. Colin Powell joined the ROTC and discovered the world of the soldier. This world would become his life.

GROWING UP
IN THE BRONX

In 1926, Maud Ariel McKoy said good-bye to the beautiful blue-green sea surrounding her native Jamaica. She was heading to New York City. Jamaica is an island in the Caribbean Sea, southeast of the United States. Today, it is an independent nation, but at that time, Jamaica belonged to Great Britain. Jamaica had poor living conditions. There were not many good jobs for the people who lived there. Many Jamaicans left their homeland and came to cities like New York.

Maud and her mother sailed together to New York City. They settled in Harlem, a community where many black people live. Harlem is in Manhattan, the central borough, or section, of the city. Maud and her mother found work as dressmakers.

Another Jamaican, Luther Theophilus Powell, had arrived in the United States a few months before. Luther had found work in Connecticut. On Sundays, Luther Powell went to church at St. Phillip's Episcopal

In the 1920s, when Colin Powell's parents arrived, Harlem was a social and cultural center for African Americans in New York.

Church in Harlem, where Maud McKoy also attended services. Luther introduced himself to Maud in the summer of 1927 at a church picnic. By 1929, the pair were making wedding plans.

It was a difficult time to start a new life together. On October 27, 1929, a worldwide economic crisis called the Great Depression began. Many companies went out of business. Millions of Americans lost their jobs, and some even lost their homes.

On December 28, 1929, Luther and Maud Powell were married. When they came back from their honeymoon, they found the companies they worked for had gone out of business. The Powells were now out of work. Luckily, they had a place to live, at 20 Morningside Avenue in Harlem, and food to eat. Soon, they found new jobs. In 1931, the Powells had their first child, a girl they named Marilyn. On April 5, 1937, Colin Luther Powell was born.

Colin's parents were hardworking people. All the money they earned went to support their children. Luther Powell was a shipping clerk. He often would not get home until seven or eight o'clock at night. Maud Powell worked at home for a clothing company. She was always busy sewing clothes in the kitchen.

Still, Colin's parents found time for their children. They read the newspapers aloud to them every day. On Sundays they all went to church together. Work and family—those were the two things that were most important to the Powells.

When Colin was five, the Powells moved from Harlem to the South Bronx, another borough of New York City. In the 1940s, the Bronx was a step up from Harlem. It also had better schools for Colin and Marilyn. The family lived in an apartment at 952 Kelly Street. The other tenants in the building were mostly Jewish, Irish, and Italian. The neighborhood also had many Puerto Ricans and African Americans. When he was growing up, Colin says, "I didn't know I was a minority because everybody there was a minority." It was a safe neighborhood, where everyone looked out

Young Colin Powell learned the values of family, education, and hard work from his parents. Here, he poses with his father, sister, and mother.

for one another. The air was filled with the sound of different languages and the smells of exotic foods. The elevated subway line rumbled above the stores.

Colin was much too young to remember the Great Depression, but he does remember World War II. Colin was four years old when the Japanese bombed the United States Naval Base at Pearl Harbor, Hawaii, in December 1941. It was then that the United States entered the war. Colin began hearing his parents talk about the Army and the Navy. Colin did not really know what World War II was about. But he had seen

The United States was involved in World War II from 1941 to 1945. Colin Powell's childhood was filled with news of the fighting in Europe and the Far East.

pictures of his cousin, James Lopez Watson, who was a soldier stationed in Italy. Colin imagined being a soldier in a faraway place. He played soldier with his friends, carrying a stick as if it were a gun.

At other times, Colin played stickball and rode bicycles. He liked to eat franks and burgers at a nearby fast-food restaurant. On Saturdays, he and his friends would see movies for 25 cents at the Tiffany Theater. Colin loved Westerns and thrillers. He also often spent time with his aunts, uncles, and cousins.

Colin and Marilyn went to Public School 39 in the South Bronx. Colin was not a very good student. Studying did not interest him. What did interest him was finding out how things worked. He loved to take things apart and put them back together.

Once, when he was eight, Colin played hooky from school. He made the mistake of coming home before school let out. A neighbor quickly reported him to his parents. That night Colin got a lecture about honesty and education. Maud and Luther Powell knew that the first step to success was education.

In the fifth grade, Colin was placed in the "slow," or bottom, class. Although Colin was not a strong student, in other ways he was a good child. He was always pleasant. Everyone liked him. His parents made a deal with him. If Colin would pass his subjects, go to college, and get a good job, they would be happy. Colin agreed.

At Morris High School in the Bronx, Colin still got no more than average grades. He fooled around just as all teenagers do, but he never got into trouble. He joined the Morris High School track team. Colin also worked to earn pocket money by fixing cribs and carriages at Sickser's children's furniture store.

Colin was 16 when he graduated from Morris High in 1953. He still did not know what his career would be. He knew he wanted to attend New York University or the City College of New York (CCNY). Although both schools accepted him, Colin picked CCNY because it cost only ten dollars a year to go there. It was at CCNY that young Colin Powell would discover his life's work.

Chapter ## Three

MATURING IN THE ARMY

Colin Powell enrolled at CCNY in February of 1954. Early in his first semester, Colin noticed some fellow students wearing nice-looking uniforms with fancy decorations. It looked like they were in some kind of special club. He found out that these students were cadets in the Reserve Officers' Training Corps, or ROTC. ROTC is a program that trains students to become Army officers. Colin noticed that some of the cadets wore a special cord on their uniforms. He learned that the students in these uniforms belonged to the Pershing Rifles, a special part of the ROTC. The Pershing Rifles were a precision drill team. This meant that they had to learn complicated marching steps.

In the fall of his freshman year, Colin excitedly joined the ROTC and became a member of the Pershing Rifles. At first, Colin only joined so he could wear the uniform and get attention from young women. Soon, however, Colin learned that there were

Colin Powell first put on a uniform in 1954, when he joined the ROTC at City College of New York.

many good things about being in the military. Military people got a steady income. The military also paid their college tuition. Colin began to like the idea of a military career.

Colin got C's in most of his classroom subjects. Yet in all his ROTC courses, he got A's. "When you find something you're good at, you tend to pursue it," he said later.

Soon, Colin's uniform began to mean responsibility. That made him feel good, and he worked hard at being a good cadet. In fact, he was eventually chosen to be commander of the Pershing Rifles. A cousin and ROTC classmate of Colin's recalled: "Even back then,

Colin drew attention when he entered a room. You just knew he would become a leader."

Summer military training was an important part of the ROTC program. Colin was sent to Fort Bragg, North Carolina, for this training. It was the mid-1950s. In those days, laws in most southern states enforced segregation, or separation by race. Fort Bragg was very segregated. The white community near Fort Bragg did not like having African-American soldiers nearby. It was here that Colin saw racial tension for the first time in his life. He saw "colored only" and "white only" signs at water fountains and restrooms. He saw that

At Fort Bragg in North Carolina, young Colin Powell had his first experience of military life and of serious racial tension.

white officers and African-American officers had separate officers' clubs. These things made him angry.

Members of the military were not allowed to join protests. If Colin wanted to help his fellow African Americans, he would have to do it within the Army. Colin began reading about other African Americans who had served in the military. One was Henry Ossiah Flipper. In 1877, he had been the first black graduate of the United States Military Academy at West Point, New York. During his four years there, he often faced the racism of his classmates. Later, Lieutenant Flipper was discharged from the Army just because he was black. Eighty years later, long after he was dead, the Army **reinstated** him honorably.

Another notable African-American military man was Benjamin O. Davis. In 1940, he became the first black man to be promoted to brigadier general in the U.S. Army. Davis's son, Benjamin O. Davis, Jr., was also a strong achiever in the military. In 1936, he became the second black cadet to graduate from West Point— 59 years after Lieutenant Flipper! For the first year he was there, Davis's classmates had refused to speak to him because he was black. Benjamin Davis, Jr., became a general like his father. All of these African-American military men were strong examples for Colin Powell. He saw that he could stand up to racism and still make a difference.

On June 9, 1958, Colin Powell graduated from CCNY with a bachelor's degree in geology, the science

By the time Colin Powell graduated from CCNY in 1958, he had discovered his life's work as a soldier in the United States Army.

of the Earth. He had graduated at the top of his class in ROTC and earned the rank of cadet colonel. After graduation, Colin joined the Army. He accepted a commission, or assignment, as a second lieutenant in the **infantry**. He was now Second Lieutenant Powell, United States Army.

Four

WINNING
RESPECT

Second Lieutenant Powell reported to Fort Benning, Georgia, where he began taking very tough training courses. One was the Infantry Officer's Training course, where Colin learned to command soldiers. Another course was the Airborne and Ranger School, where he learned to parachute, fight without weapons, and survive in the wilderness.

Ranger training was very hard. Colin and his fellow soldiers were sent out into the wilderness alone. It rained all the time and the ground was muddy. The soldiers had to wade through swamps and climb down steep cliffs using ropes. When they got hungry, they had to find plants and animals safe enough to cook and eat. Even though it was hard work, Colin liked it. He was tough and strong. He cheered up his fellow soldiers when they were tired, cold, and dirty.

Soon after he completed his training, Second

Lieutenant Powell's first real assignment came in October 1958, when he was 21. He was sent to West Germany, where many U.S. soldiers were stationed. The American soldiers were in West Germany to protect Europe from the Soviet Union, which was a very powerful Communist country.

Second Lieutenant Powell was commander of a platoon, a military unit of about forty soldiers. As a new officer, he did not want his soldiers to be afraid of him. His fairness and concern made him very popular. Although he missed his family, Colin enjoyed his first experience in a foreign country. He was even promoted to first lieutenant. In 1960, Colin was sent back to the United States.

While Colin was stationed at Fort Devens, in Massachusetts, a friend of his set him up for a blind date. Colin was a little nervous. He had never even seen this woman. Suppose she did not like him? Suppose he did not like her? Colin's date was Alma Vivian Johnson, from Birmingham, Alabama. Most of the people in her family were teachers and business professionals. Alma herself was studying to be an audiologist, a professional who helps people with hearing problems.

For both Alma and Colin, it was love at first sight. Two years later, on August 24, 1962, Colin Powell and Alma Johnson were married. They moved into an apartment on the Army base at Fort Devens. At first, it seemed like it would be a quiet year. It turned out, however, to be a very eventful one.

For Colin and Alma Powell, love at first sight led to a marriage that is still strong after over thirty years.

Again, Colin had been promoted, this time to the rank of captain. Four months after his wedding, Captain Powell received orders to report to Fort Bragg, North Carolina. There he would prepare to go to Vietnam, a country in Southeast Asia. In those days, few Americans had heard of it.

At that time, Vietnam was divided into two countries. One was North Vietnam, which was Communist. The other was South Vietnam, which was not Communist and was an ally of the United States. The two countries were at war. The United States wanted to help South Vietnam and began to send soldiers there. Some members of the U.S. military acted as advisers to

South Vietnam's president. In 1962, Captain Powell became one of those advisers.

Colin's job meant training the South Vietnamese military. He had to go into the fields and jungles with the South Vietnamese soldiers and teach them about fighting. It was dangerous work. Often Captain Powell and the South Vietnamese soldiers had to patrol through soggy, muddy rice paddies, the wetland where rice is grown. Mosquitoes buzzed around them. Bloodsucking worms called leeches crawled onto their legs. Sometimes Colin was so tired and hot that

By the middle of the 1960s, thousands of U.S. troops would be involved in the war in Vietnam.

he felt he could not go on, but he always kept on going.

One day in 1963, Captain Powell was patrolling in a rice paddy. Suddenly, he stepped into an enemy booby trap. It was made of sharpened bamboo sticks buried in the ground with the points sticking out. One of these sticks went through Colin's foot. Even though he was injured, Captain Powell had a job to do. His unit had to reach another group of soldiers that needed help. Despite his pain, Powell finished the job. Afterward, he was taken to a military hospital for surgery. Shortly after this event, Captain Powell was awarded two medals. One was the Purple Heart, for soldiers wounded in action. The other was a Bronze Star, for bravery.

By this time, people back in the United States had begun to disagree about the war in Vietnam. Some people did not want the U.S. involved in the war. Even though Colin knew that it was a very unpopular war, he was still a soldier. If his country needed him, he was ready to serve.

When Colin left for Vietnam, Alma had returned to Birmingham to stay with her parents. In 1963, she gave birth to a son, Michael. At the time, Captain Powell was deep in the swamps of Vietnam, suffering from diarrhea, mosquitoes, and leeches. He was leading a combat unit under intense enemy fire. It was two weeks before Colin Powell got the message that he was now a father.

Finally, after almost a year in Vietnam, Captain

Powell returned to the United States. He was stationed at Fort Benning. For a while after Colin's return, Alma and Michael stayed in Birmingham. On weekends, Colin traveled to Birmingham to be with them.

Colin was uncomfortable in Birmingham. Every day there was racial violence. The Civil Rights Movement had begun. Under the leadership of Dr. Martin Luther King, Jr., and other activists, African Americans were protesting segregation. Many whites were fighting back. "I was stunned, disheartened and angry," Colin would later recall. "While I had been fighting in Vietnam alongside brave soldiers trying to preserve their freedom, in my own land a long-simmering conflict had turned into an open fight in our streets and cities—a fight that had to be won."

Colin was happy to get his family to Fort Benning. The family soon included a daughter, Linda, born in 1965. In 1966, Colin Powell was promoted to major. The following year, Major Powell was assigned to Fort Leavenworth, Kansas. Colin knew that he needed to go back to school if he wanted more promotions. So he signed up to take advanced courses at the Army Command and General Staff College. Here, he worked much harder at his studies than he had in high school and college. Colin Powell graduated second in a class of 1,244 students.

Meanwhile, the war in Vietnam grew worse. Hundreds of American soldiers were dying there every day. In 1968, Major Powell was sent back to Vietnam.

Civil Rights protestors were often met with violent responses. Here, firefighters use hoses to break up a peaceful protest in Birmingham, Alabama.

There, he became the executive officer of a battalion, a unit of 500 to 1,000 soldiers. His job was to train soldiers for combat. Because of Colin's strong performance in school, his picture was printed in the Army's newspaper. The commander of his division saw the newspaper article and was shocked. "I've got the number two Leavenworth graduate in my division, and he's stuck in the boonies?" he shouted. The commander wanted Colin on his own staff. Major Powell was quickly recalled from the field and put to work as operations officer for the division. This was thought to be a much safer job than working in the field—but it was not.

One day, Major Powell was traveling by helicopter. The pilot tried to land in a small area. Suddenly the propeller hit a tree, and the chopper crashed and caught on fire. Colin jumped out of the wreckage. Then he saw that others were still trapped inside. Blinded and choking from the smoke, he went back four times to carry the men to safety. As Colin got the last man out, the chopper exploded in a huge ball of fire. For risking his own safety and saving the lives of others, Colin received the soldier's medal.

Major Powell left Vietnam in July 1969. He was only 32 years old, but he was already a highly rated officer. When he returned to the United States, he enrolled in graduate school at George Washington University in Washington, D.C. The Powells' third child, Annemarie, was born during the following year. Colin was soon promoted to lieutenant colonel. The next year, he earned his master's degree in business administration. He quickly got a high-level position in Washington. In his new job, Colin helped to manage the country's defense budget.

In 1972, Colin got a call from an Army personnel officer. He wanted Colin to apply for a White House Fellowship. White House Fellows are bright men and women from many different fields of work. Each year, several are chosen to be assistants in government offices. Colin—and 1,499 others—applied to be White House Fellows. Colin was one of 17 picked.

As a White House Fellow, Colin was assigned to the

Office of Management and Budget, located right next to the White House. At that time, Richard Nixon was President. Colin's bosses were Caspar Weinberger, the director of the office, and his deputy, or assistant, Frank Carlucci.

Colin quickly impressed his bosses. He also liked this job. He was making policy and setting goals for the military. Here, he could combine his business knowledge and his military knowledge to serve his country. Colin Powell was also learning how the U.S. government works, from the inside.

Colin Powell's family would support him throughout his military career. Here, he poses with his three children, Annemarie, Michael, and Linda, and his wife, Alma, in 1987.

Chapter Five

HELPING PRESIDENTS

When Colin Powell completed his fellowship in 1973, the Army had a special assignment for him. Lieutenant Colonel Powell was sent to Seoul, South Korea. A battalion of American soldiers stationed there was getting out of hand. Some of the soldiers were using drugs, and there were fights between black and white soldiers. Colin's job in Seoul was to solve these problems as quickly as possible.

Colin explained what he did. "I threw the bums out of the Army and put the drug users in jail," he said. Colin made the rest of the soldiers run four miles every morning. By night time, Colin said, "they were too tired to get into any trouble." Within months, the problems in the battalion had disappeared. Both blacks and whites praised Colin for his fairness.

Lieutenant Colonel Powell's success in Korea earned him another job in Washington in 1974. This time, it was in the Office of the Assistant Secretary of

Colin Powell's special assignment in Korea drew on his skills as a leader and a problem solver.

Defense, which advises the President on all matters involving national defense. Colin's job was to decide what training Army soldiers would need over the next ten years. For a year, he did research on the subject and wrote reports.

In 1975, Colin enrolled at the National War College to learn more about the history of war. The next year, he graduated with honors. He was soon promoted to full colonel. Over the next three years, Colin advised officials in the Department of Defense. In 1979, he became a brigadier general, with a silver star on his uniform. In 1982, Colin returned to Fort Leavenworth to run the base.

However, Brigadier General Powell was now in great demand around Washington. According to John Kester, one of his bosses, Colin was a strong person who understood how the government worked. "He was equally comfortable… when he was talking with a private, a general, or a president." By this time, Powell's old bosses had been promoted, too. Now Casper Weinberger was secretary of defense, and Frank Carlucci was deputy secretary of defense. The two men worked closely with President Ronald Reagan, planning military policy. They wanted Colin to work with them again.

Colin Powell was not interested in going back to office work. He wanted to serve his country in active military service. That was where his training and strengths were. But Weinberger convinced him that he could best serve his country by working for the Defense Department. So Colin and his family returned to Washington. In July 1983, Brigadier General Powell became military adviser to Carlucci and senior military assistant to Weinberger. In August, he was promoted to major general. This meant a second star on his uniform.

Major General Powell's job was to inform the White House and other government departments about all military operations. Colin was at his desk at six-thirty every morning. During the day, he worked on the daily budget reports of the country's trillion-dollar weapons program. That meant he decided how

Colin Powell was happiest when he was in uniform, serving his country through active military service.

much money should go into each part of the program. Colin seldom left his office before seven o'clock at night. His hard work won him respect and trust.

Once again, however, the Army called Colin back to field duty. In June 1986, the Army asked Colin to take over the V Corps, or "Fifth" Corps, in West Germany. He would be in command of a force of over 70,000 soldiers. This was Colin's dream come true. It was also special because Colin's son Michael, now 25 years old and a lieutenant in the Army, was in West Germany. The Powells packed up and moved once again. Soon, Colin Powell became a lieutenant general and received his third star.

Just six months after the family had settled in Germany, Colin received a phone call. The White House wanted him back! This time, it was to help

Frank Carlucci. Carlucci was now the new **national security** adviser. This meant he was the President's closest adviser on foreign policy.

"No way," Colin replied. He had already spent too much of his career in Washington. Commanding the V Corps was the best job he had ever had. He did not want to give it up.

Several nights later, the Powells' phone rang again. This time it was President Reagan. "I know you've been looking forward to this command," he said. "But we need you here." Lieutenant General Powell hated to turn down the President of the United States. He accepted the position.

The Powells came back to Washington. They had now moved almost twenty times in twenty years! At a Washington press conference in January 1987, Lieutenant General Powell explained his decision. "I'm a serviceman, a soldier, and it looked like my service might be of greater use here." Colin's new job was deputy national security adviser. This meant that he would advise the President on when to use military force. He would also tell the President the costs and results of military action.

When Lieutenant General Powell arrived in Washington, it was a bad time for the White House. Officials in the White House were accused of breaking the law. First, they had secretly sold weapons to Iran. Then they had sent the money they made to a group called the Contras, which was fighting against the

Colin was often recalled from field duty to take high-level jobs in Washington, advising government leaders.

government of Nicaragua, in Central America. These actions went against laws that had been passed by Congress. The matter became known as the Iran-Contra scandal.

Congress brought charges against many people who had advised President Reagan. Some were convicted for breaking the law. Colin Powell was not one of them. No charges were brought against him. He was one of the few people close to the President whose reputation was not damaged by the scandal.

At this time, the Powells got frightening news from West Germany. Michael Powell had been in a bad jeep accident. His pelvis was broken in six places. At the base hospital, Michael fought for his life for four days.

On November 5, 1987, General Colin Powell accepted the job of national security adviser. He was joined at a special White House ceremony by former Defense Secretary Caspar Weinberger, President Ronald Reagan, and new Defense Secretary Frank Carlucci.

He was then flown to Walter Reed Army Medical Center in Washington for surgery. Doctors were afraid that he would need to use a wheelchair for the rest of his life.

The Powell family gave Michael all their love and support. "You'll make it," Colin told his son. "You want to make it, so you will make it!" A year and a half after the accident, Michael could walk with a cane. In the next two years, he got married and had a son. He soon enrolled in law school. Colin was proud of his son's recovery and hard work.

In 1987, Colin's boss, Frank Carlucci, was promoted to secretary of defense. When the President asked his advisers who should get Carlucci's job as national security adviser, Colin Powell's name was the only one mentioned. On November 5, President Reagan appointed Colin Powell national security adviser. Colin's appointment made front-page news all over the country. He became the first African-American national security adviser in U.S. history. Colin Powell wanted to be judged by his actions, not his color. Still, he was very proud to be the first African American in that position.

Colin Powell was now at the very center of power in Washington. He often served as a spokesman for the nation's military efforts. Colin got up early every morning to read a thick pile of military reports from all around the world. Afterward, he met with President Reagan to discuss national security. To show his appreciation for Colin's hard work, President Reagan promoted Colin to a full four-star general.

In 1988, George Bush, was elected President. President Bush told General Powell that he liked and respected him, but he wanted someone else to be his national security adviser. Colin Powell was out of a job—but not for long.

Chapter  Six

A NATIONAL HERO

Geneneral Powell quickly received two job offers. The first offer was from the army chief of staff, who wanted to make Colin head of United States Forces Command. The second offer was from a publishing agent in New York. The agent told Powell that he could make as much as a million dollars a year just giving speeches around the country. Maybe he could write a book, too.

Colin could not decide. He took out a piece of paper and divided it into two columns: "Reasons to Stay in the Army" and "Reasons to Leave the Army." In the first column, he wrote down a dozen reasons to stay. In the second, he could only come up with one reason to leave: money. That was not a good enough reason for Colin Powell.

After talking with his family and friends, Colin decided to stay in the Army. He took the job as head of the U.S. Forces Command at Fort McPherson in

In August 1989, George Bush appointed Colin Powell Chairman of the Joint Chiefs of Staff, the highest military post in the United States.

Atlanta, Georgia. However, Colin would not stay in his new job very long. In early August 1989, four months after arriving in Atlanta, General Powell got a call from President Bush. The Chairman of the Joint Chiefs of Staff, Admiral William Crowe, was retiring. The President wanted to appoint Colin as the new Chairman of the Joint Chiefs of Staff.

The Joint Chiefs of Staff includes all the leaders of the Army, Navy, Marines, and Air Force. They plan the military operations of the United States. Three times a week, these leaders meet secretly in the defense building, called the Pentagon. They sit in a tightly

As Chairman of the Joint Chiefs of Staff, Colin Powell led the heads of the Army, Navy, Marines, and Air Force in planning military strategy.

guarded room without windows, called the "tank." Not even the president knows what is said in that room.

The Chairman is the leader of the Joint Chiefs of Staff. He is the top supervisor of everyone in the armed forces, and the main military adviser to the president. It is the highest military position in the country. In a ceremony on August 11, 1989, President Bush said Colin Powell would "bring leadership, insight, and wisdom to our efforts to keep our military strong and ready." Colin responded, "Mr. President, I am ready to go to it." At 52, Powell was the youngest Chairman of the Joint Chiefs of Staff ever to serve.

African Americans were especially proud that General Powell was now the country's top soldier. He was higher in rank and power than any other African

American in U.S. history. And Colin always remained proud of his roots. In a speech to African-American reporters, General Powell said that his "appointment would never have been possible without the sacrifices of those black soldiers who served this great nation in war for nearly 300 years."

Colin's new office was in the Pentagon. His awards hung on the wall behind his desk. On another wall was a painting of one of Colin's heroes, Lieutenant Henry O. Flipper. On his desk, Colin kept a list of rules he used every day, including: "Get mad, then get over it;" "Share credit;" and "Have a vision. Be demanding."

Only two days after Colin took his new position, his military skills were needed once again. Soldiers in the country of Panama, in Central America, were trying to overthrow their leader, General Manuel Noriega. Noriega was a dictator, a leader who kept all the power in his own hands. He had also been accused of crimes, such as smuggling drugs. The Panamanian soldiers begged for help from the United States, but the United States had made no plans to get involved. At first, General Powell said no to their plea.

Some people did not like the way Colin dealt with the problem in Panama. Colin did not let it upset him. Instead, he sat down with his generals and began planning the largest U.S. invasion since the Vietnam War. President Bush agreed with General Powell's plan.

On December 15, 1989, Noriega declared a "state of war" with the United States. General Powell and his team acted swiftly. Their mission was called Operation Just Cause. Colin sent 26,000 American soldiers to Panama. They quickly defeated Noriega's army. Noriega was captured and arrested on drug charges. Then he was taken to an American prison in Florida. The mission was a success.

Things did not settle down for long. In 1990, Colin was again planning for war. This time, it was on the other side of the world, with a country called Iraq. Iraq is in the Middle East, near a body of water called the Persian Gulf. Iraq and the countries near it have a large supply of oil. Iraq's president, Saddam Hussein, had become angry at the neighboring country of Kuwait. On August 2, 1990, Saddam Hussein's troops invaded Kuwait and took over the government. Some people believed that Iraq was getting ready to take over other countries in the Persian Gulf region. If that happened, Saddam Hussein would control most of the world's oil supply.

General Powell and another Army general, Norman Schwarzkopf, went to work. Their goal was to defend the oil fields from Iraqi attack. They also wanted Iraq to remove its troops from Kuwait. The plan was called Operation Desert Shield. It would involve the largest, fastest movement of American soldiers in history. President Bush left the planning of the military operation completely in Colin's hands.

By the end of September, France, Britain, Egypt, Syria, and 24 other countries had promised to send soldiers to the Persian Gulf to help the United States. Just after New Year's Day, 1991, President Bush offered Saddam Hussein one last chance to get his troops out of Kuwait. Three days later, Congress voted to give the President the power to begin a war.

At 4:50 P.M., on January 16, the first fighter planes took off to begin what was called Operation Desert Storm. General Powell used Stealth bombers to attack Saddam Hussein's army. These bombers are special

General Colin Powell talks with General Norman Schwarzkopf, commander of the Operation Desert Storm forces. Both men became national heroes.

Colin Powell's leadership helped the United States achieve victory in the Gulf War. Here, he gives a briefing on the war at the Pentagon.

high-tech planes, difficult for the enemy to detect. The Iraqi forces quickly began their retreat.

By early March, the Iraqi army was completely defeated. Iraq agreed to surrender and get out of Kuwait. Generals Powell and Schwarzkopf were heroes. Congress had a special gold medal made for each of them. In May, President Bush appointed General Powell to another two-year term as Chairman of the Joint Chiefs of Staff.

After the Gulf War, General Powell returned to his old high school, Morris High School, in the South

Bronx. He also took a tour of Kelly Street, where he had once lived. To the Morris High School students, he said, "Stick with it. Stay in high school and get the diploma. Don't think you are limited by your background. Challenges are there to be knocked down."

General Powell finally retired from the military on September 30, 1993. He had completed his two terms as Chairman of the Joint Chiefs of Staff. But Colin Powell's achievements continued. He wrote his autobiography, or life story, entitled *My American Journey*. It was published in 1995. He receives many invitations to speak all over the country. In his spare time, Colin Powell continues to read about military history. He still enjoys watching Westerns and horror movies. He also still loves taking things apart and fixing them—including old cars.

Colin's services as a problem solver are still very important, too. In 1994, former U.S. President Jimmy Carter contacted Colin and asked him to be part of a negotiating team to solve the crisis in Haiti. The United States was ready to invade the island nation by force. Carter's team would make one last effort to avoid bloodshed. Colin learned that many of the Haitian soldiers had been trained at Fort Bragg and Fort Benning, the same places he had trained. So he knew how to speak to them soldier-to-soldier. He made Haitian general Raoul Cedras promise there would be no resistance when the U.S. troops arrived. The promise was kept. Within weeks, Haitian president Jean-Bertrand Aristide was back in power.

Colin Powell is a man of both war and peace. His negotiating skills helped keep the peace in Haiti in 1994.

Colin Powell's ability to work well with leaders and to get good results have impressed millions of Americans. They have even convinced some people that Colin Powell should run for President or Vice-President of the United States.

Today, Colin especially likes to focus his attention on young people. He says he hopes young people will see him and think, "'Hey, look at that dude. He came out of the South Bronx. If he got out, why can't I?'"

In his speeches, General Colin Powell tells young African Americans that there is no substitute for hard work and study. He also urges them not to allow racism to affect their feelings about themselves. "Don't let your blackness, your minority status, be a problem to you," he advises them. "Let it be a problem to someone else. You can't change it. Don't think everybody is staring at you because you're black. It may be true, but let that be their problem, not yours."

Important Dates

1937   Born on April 5, in Harlem, an area of New York City

1954   Joins the ROTC program at CCNY.

1958   Graduates college with a degree in geology and the rank of second lieutenant in the U.S. Army.

1962   Marries Alma Johnson. Sent to Vietnam.

1968   Takes second assignment in Vietnam.

1971   Earns master's degree in business administration.

1972   Becomes a White House Fellow in Washington, D.C.

1973   Completes a special assignment in Korea.

1983   Becomes senior military assistant to the secretary of defense.

1987   Appointed national security adviser by President Reagan.

1989   Appointed Chairman of the Joint Chiefs of Staff by President Bush. Oversees mission in Panama.

1991   Helps command successful attack against Iraq in the Persian Gulf War.

1993   Retires from the military.

1994   Helps negotiate the peaceful return to power of the president of Haiti.

Glossary

cadets Young people, usually students, training to be military officers.

infantry A group of soldiers who fight on foot.

invasion When an army enters a country, usually by force.

national security A country's safety from enemies.

negotiating Dealing with a problem through discussion.

reinstated Restored to previous position and rank.

Bibliography

Blue, Rose, and Corinne J. Nadeau. *Colin Powell: Straight to the Top*. Brookfield, CT: The Millbrook Press, 1991.

Haskins, Jim. *Colin Powell: A Biography*. New York: Scholastic, 1992.

Rowan, Carl T. "Called to Service: The Colin Powell Story." *Reader's Digest*, December 1989.

Senna, Carl. *Colin Powell: A Man of War and Peace*. New York: Walker, 1992.

Index

Airborne and Ranger School, 19
Aristide, Jean-Bertrand, 5, 6, 43

Birmingham, 20, 23, 24, 25
Bronx, New York 6, 10, 12, 13, 43, 44
Bronze Star, 23
Bush, George, 35, 37, 38, 39, 40, 41, 42

Carlucci, Frank, 27, 30, 32, 34, 35
Carter, Jimmy, 5, 43
Cedras, Raoul, 6, 43
City College of New York, 13-15, 17, 18
Civil Rights Movement, 24, 25

Davis, Benjamin O., 17
Davis, Benjamin O., Jr., 17

V ("Fifth") Corps, 31, 32
Flipper, Henry Ossiah, 17, 39
Fort Benning, 19, 24, 43
Fort Bragg, 16, 21, 43
Fort Devens, 20
Fort Leavenworth, 24, 29
Fort McPherson, 36

Haiti, 5, 6, 43
Harlem, 8, 9, 10, 46
Hussein, Saddam, 40, 41

Infantry Officer's Training course, 19
Iran-Contra scandal, 32-33
Iraq, 40-42

Jamaica, 6, 8
Joint Chiefs of Staff, 37-38

Korea, 28, 29
Kuwait, 40, 41, 42

Morris High School, 13, 43

National War College, 29
Noriega, Manuel, 39, 40

Office of Management and Budget, 27
Operation Desert Storm, 6, 40-42
Operation Just Cause, 40

Panama, 39, 40
Pentagon, 37, 39
Pershing Rifles, 14, 15
Persian Gulf War, 6, 40-42
Powell, Alma Vivian (Johnson), 20, 21, 23, 24, 27
Powell, Annemarie, 26, 27
Powell, Colin Luther,
    as a young officer, 18-20
    as Chairman of the Joint Chiefs of Staff, 6, 37-43
    as head of the U.S. Forces Command, 36
    as national security adviser, 6, 34-35
    as White House Fellow, 26-27
    college years of, 7, 13-18
    early Defense Department career of, 6, 28-31
    early life of, 6, 10-13
    family life of, 6, 10-13, 20, 23, 24, 26, 27, 33-35
    graduate studies of, 26, 29
    post-retirement activity of, 5, 43-45
    Vietnam War service of, 21-23, 24-26
Powell, Linda, 24, 27
Powell, Luther Theophilus, 8-9, 10, 11, 13
Powell, Marilyn, 10, 11, 12
Powell, Maud Ariel (McKoy), 8-9, 10, 11, 13
Powell, Michael, 23, 24, 27, 31, 33-35

Reagan, Ronald, 30, 32, 33, 34, 35
Reserve Officers' Training Corps (ROTC), 7, 14, 15, 16, 18

Schwarzkopf, Norman, 40, 41, 42

United States Army, 11, 14, 17, 18, 20, 24, 25, 26, 28, 29, 31, 36, 38, 40-42
United States Department of Defense, 29, 30

Vietnam War, 21-23, 24-26, 40

Washington, D.C., 26, 28, 30, 32, 33, 34, 35
Weinberger, Caspar, 27, 30, 34
West Germany, 20, 31, 33
White House, 26, 27, 30, 31, 32, 34